W9-AHY-718

READING POWER

Dale Earnhardt, Jr.
NASCAR Road Racer

Rob Kirkpatrick

The Rosen Publishing Group's
PowerKids Press ™
New York

1

121 68647

For my grandmother, Irene.

Published in 2000 by The Rosen Publishing Group, Inc.
29 East 21st Street, New York, NY 10010

Copyright © 2000 by The Rosen Publishing Group, Inc.

All rights reserved. No part of this book may be reproduced in any form without permission in writing from the publisher, except by a reviewer.

First Edition

Book design: Maria Melendez

Photo Credits: pp. 5, 22 © Jamie Squire/Allsport; pp. 7, 9, 11, 21 © David Taylor/Allsport; p. 13 © Craig Jones; pp. 15, 17 © Jon Ferrey/Allsport; p. 19 © Matthew Stockman/Allsport.

Text Consultant: Linda J. Kirkpatrick, Reading Specialist/Reading Recovery Teacher

Kirkpatrick, Rob.
      Dale Earnhardt, Jr. : NASCAR road racer / by Rob Kirkpatrick.
      p. cm. — (Reading power)
    Includes index.
    SUMMARY: A simple introduction to the NASCAR driver who is the son of another winning racer, Dale Earnhardt, Sr.
      ISBN 0-8239-5545-1 (lib. bdg.)
      1. Earnhardt, Dale, Jr. Juvenile literature. 2. Automobile racing drivers—United States Biography Juvenile literature. [1. Earnhardt, Dale, Jr. 2. Automobile racing drivers.] I. Title. II. Series.
      GV1032.E18 K57 1999
      796.72'092—dc21
      [B]   99-32384
                                                      CIP

Manufactured in the United States of America

Contents

1 Meet Dale Earnhardt, Jr.   4

2 Car Number 3   8

3 Pit Stop   14

4 A Big Race   18

5 Books and Web Sites   23

6 Glossary   24

7 Index/Word Count   24

8 Note   24

Dale Earnhardt, Jr. races cars.

The cars in races have numbers on them. Dale had a car with number 31.

Dale has number 3 on his car now. He drives a Chevrolet.

9

Some cars can get very close in a race. Dale likes his car to be in front.

Lots of people like to see Dale race. They like to see him drive fast.

People help Dale in races. He makes a pit stop when he needs help with his car.

Sometimes, Dale needs new tires. New tires can help Dale drive fast.

In 1998, Dale won a big race. The race was the Diehard 250.

19

Dale needs to have a helmet, goggles, and a mike for his races.

Dale's father races cars, too. His name is Dale also.

Here are more books to read about the Earnhardts:

Dale Earnhardt, Jr. (NASCAR Track Sounds)
Futech Interactive Products

Dale Earnhardt, Sr. (NASCAR Track Sounds)
Futech Interactive Products

To learn more about NASCAR, check out this Web site:

http://sikids.com/racing/overdrive/index.html

Glossary

Chevrolet (shev-roh-LAY) The name of a type of car.
pit stop (PIT STOP) When a driver goes off the track to get his car fixed.
goggles (GAH-gulz) What a driver wears to keep his eyes safe.
helmet (HEL-mit) What a driver wears to keep his head safe.
mike (MYK) What a driver uses so he can talk to his crew while driving.

Index

C
Chevrolet, 8

D
Diehard 250, 18
drive, 8, 12, 16

G
goggles, 20

H
helmet, 20
help, 14

P
people, 12, 14
pit stop, 14

T
tires, 16

Word Count: 129

Note to Librarians, Teachers, and Parents

If reading is a challenge, Reading Power is a solution! Reading Power is perfect for readers who want high-interest subject matter at an accessible reading level. These fact-filled, photo-illustrated books are designed for readers who want straightforward vocabulary, engaging topics, and a manageable reading experience. With clear picture/text correspondence, leveled Reading Power books put the reader in charge. Now readers have the power to get the information they want and the skills they need in a user-friendly format.